Les Hautes Roches
(Photo Patrick Verbeeck)

With special thanks to our photographers

Jan Dirkx
Phile Deprez
Sven Everaert
Vincent Gyselinck
Patrick Verbeeck

&

Paul Kusseneers
Concept & Lay-Out

&

Printed by de Plano

More information on all our books you find on our website :
www.d-publications.com

Compiled by :Luc Quisenaerts
Concept & lay-out: Paul Kusseneers
Printed by: De Plano
English Edition: Anne & Owen Davis
Publishers: D-Publications
List of photographers:
<u>Jan Dirkx:</u> La Verniaz et ses Chalets, Bernard Loiseau La Côte d'Or, Château de Courcelles, Les Hautes Roches, Domaine des Hauts de Loire, Château de Curzay, Les Deux Abbesses,
<u>Phile Deprez:</u> Hôtel d'Europe, La Bastide de Marie, Le Pigonnet, La Maison Troisgros, Cour des Loges
<u>Sven Everaert;</u> Montalembert, Lancaster, Lodge Parc, Le Mont Blanc
<u>Vincent Gyselinck:</u> Ferme Saint-Siméon, Les Maisons de Bricourt, Grand Hôtel des Bains, Château de Locguénolé La Riboto de Taven, Bernard Loiseau La Côte d'Or, Georges Blanc
<u>Patrick Verbeeck:</u> Le Cagnard, La Bastide Saint-Antoine, Les Muscadins, Hostellerie l'Abbaye de la Celle, Le Yaca, Club de Cavaliere, Royal Rivièra, Lodge Parc, Le Mont Blanc, La Maison Blanche,Villa Florentine, Les Sources de Caudalie, Les Hautes Roches, Domaine des Hauts de Loire.

ISBN 90-76124-34-5   D/2001/8101/11

© All rights reserved. No part of this publication may be reproduced in any way whatsoever without written permission from D-Publications.

First edition

HOTEL GEMS II
OF
FRANCE

COMPILED
AND
WRITTEN BY

LUC QUISENAERTS

PUBLISHERS D-PUBLICATIONS

THE SERIES 'HOTEL GEMS OF THE WORLD'

Dear Reader,

Each book will describe the rich and fascinating hotel heritage of a certain country, a group of countries or a continent.

Each country will be described from a very special, original angle.

By enjoying the hospitality of the people of a country for one or several nights, one can taste the history, the culture and the cuisine of such a country in a deeply personal way.

Therefore, we thank all the hotels, who co-operated in this project for offering their hospitality, which is usually reserved for the guests who stay there, to the readers of these books.

In the following months and years, we hope to offer you a whole series of new voyages of discovery to the most fascinating hotels in the world.

We intend to enable readers to 'walk' through all these gems, to discover their unique nooks and crannies, by leafing through each book.

That is why this series, and each book in itself, can be considered a valuable archive containing a piece of the wealth and beauty of a country, created by the passion of all those people who put their souls into it.

...

HOTEL GEMS II
OF
FRANCE

'Living like God in France': it has been our Leitmotif, the red thread that ran through our first book 'Hotel Gems of France', which was written some years ago now.

The immense success of the book, the enthusiastic reaction of both hoteliers and readers and the endless wealth of gastronomy, culture, history and joie de vivre of French hotels, inspired us to start a new voyage of discovery through the country, and to introduce to you a second collection of breathtakingly beautiful hotels: from the sub-tropical Mediterranean to the characteristic Breton coast at the Atlantic, from Paris, the City of Light to the eternally white crests of Mont Blanc, from the sparkling Champagne region to the famed wine castles Bordeaux.

Everywhere we found, in the people who achieved it all, the same deep passion. A passion which can not be formulated better than by hotelier Eddy Bianchini who said, when he bought Hotel Les Muscadins in Mougins in 1982 *"This is heaven! There is no reason to die now..."*

Luc Quisenaerts
Publisher

THE COLLECTION

1.	Château de Courcelles	page 10
2.	La Bastide Saint-Antoine	18
3.	Les Maisons de Bricourt	22
4.	Hôtel Mont-Blanc	28
5.	Hôtel Montalembert	32
6.	Le Yaca	38
7.	Château de Curzay	42
8.	Hostellerie de l'Abbaye de la Celle	48
9.	La Maison Troisgros	54
10.	Ferme Saint Siméon	58
11.	Les Deux Abbesses	64
12.	Château de Locguénolé	70
13.	Le Cagnard	76
14.	La Verniaz et ses Chalets	82
15.	La Maison Blanche	86
16.	Le Lodge Parc	94
17.	Domaine des Hauts de Loire	98
18.	Le Club de Cavalière	104
19.	La Bastide de Marie	108
20.	Cour des Loges	114
21.	Les Sources de Caudalie	118
22.	Hôtel d'Europe	128
23.	Les Hautes Roches	132
24.	Royal Rivièra	136
25.	Hôtel Lancaster	142
26.	Les Muscadins	148
27.	Bernard Loiseau - La Côte d'Or	152
28.	Le Pigonnet	158
29.	Grand-Hôtel des Bains	162
30.	Villa Florentine	170
31.	Georges Blanc	176
32.	La Riboto de Taven	182

Château de Courcelles

Courcelles dur Vesle, 120 kilometres from Paris, can be found in the historic triangles which is formed by Rheims, capital of Champagne, Laon (known for its cathedral and the 'Chemin des Dames') and Soissons, the city of Clovis. The 18 rooms of Château de Courcelles, which lies in a beautiful 23 hectare estate, are divided between the castle itself and the 'Vert Coeur' and 'Beau Regard' pavillions. The whole complex is in pure Louis XIV style and was built between 1690 and 1694, at the end of the rule of Louis XIV, the Sun King under whose reign Versailles, too, was built. In 1715 Louis XIV and Baron de la Grange, who built the Château de Courcelles, both died. The latter's son sold the estate to a certain Martin Bouron, Royal Notary in Paris and advisor to the King. He had two granddaughters who were known as 'Les Demoiselles de Courcelles' (the Maidens of Courcelles). Their beauty, intelligence and hospitality attracted, amongst many others, the celebrated philosopher Jean-Jacques Rousseau. During World War I the castle was occupied by the Germans. Battles fought in the area were amongst the bloodiest of the whole war and are known as 'Le Chemin des Dames'.

After the Second World War, the castle was bought by a certain Monsieur Bonjean. In the years that followed, his friend Christian Dior, the Paris fashion king, organised lavish and stylish parties at the castle. In 1988 the current owner, Bernard Anthonioz, started an ambitious renovation project and transformed the Château de Courcelles to a prestigious hotel and restaurant. And perhaps the most beautiful part of the renovation is the park, with its delightful French gardens... and a real labyrinth.

La Bastide Saint-Antoine

Opio, Peymenade, Saint Vallier... the names conjure up images of small, picturesque villages in the Grasse area, but they are also the names of the eight rooms, two junior suites and one suite at the Bastide Sainte Antoine. Each of them shows a different aspect of local charm: wood, painted in various colours, authentic furniture, floors in 18th-century terracotta... all this combined with all mod cons: terraces, bathrooms with massage baths and showers, television, a top quality hi-fi player. At the Bastide Saint Antoine, guests can enjoy a swimming pool set in completely natural surroundings, they can walk in the bucolic countryside around the hotel, or play pétanque. The hotel used to have two owners: John Taylor and industrialist Labbé de Pontamousson. Lavish parties were given here attended by celebrities such as the Kennedy family and the Rolling Stones.

The current owner, Jacques Chibois, completely renovated the Bastide, using traditional methods in order to retain the original charm of the house. Five months a year, meals are served on the Provençal terrace under the trees, in a flower-filled garden. The remaining months, guests use the restaurant, a cheerful, harmoniously decorated room with a monumental fireplace. Chef Jacques Chibois, who gained two Michelin stars, 18/20 in Gault Millau and three stars in the Bottin Gourmand, offers an intriguing cuisine based on the scents and flavours of olive oil. All these recipes are described in his book 'Parfums et Senteurs d'Huile d'Olive'.

The hotel boutique is a joy to visit, with its many regional delicacies, beauty products made with olive oil, a fashion collection signed 'Jacques Chibois' and a variety of hand-made objects. La Bastide Saint Antoine dates from the 18th century and is surrounded by magnificent countryside. It lies near Grasse, in parkland that boasts more than 400 centuries-old olive trees. Cannes is only a few minutes away, and both the restaurant and the rooms offer you a wonderful view of the Estérel massif and Théoule bay.

Les Maisons de Bricourt

"Les Maisons de Bricourt 'lives', as it were, in three places - which is most unusual in the French hotel world. There is the restaurant, my 'roots', there is 'Les Rimains', the house which we fell in love with right from the start, and our 'folly', 'La Maison Blanche'. The building which houses the restaurant dates from 1760 and was built by the Heurtaut de Bricourt family, traders who made their fortune in the 'rush' to the Far East, where it traded in silk, china and spices. It may have been our fondness for our birth house that enticed us to start our culinary adventure, and in the spring of 1982, our first clients rang the doorbell. And then there is our beloved 'Les Rimains'. In 1988 we created six rooms here, with views of the sea and the Rock of Cancale. On the far side of the Bay of Cancale stands 'Maison Richeux'. This large villa is the fulfilment of the dream of a fascinating woman. But first of all, it is interesting to tell a bit more about the origin and the history of this house. It is situated on the old Roman road that connects Saint-Malo with Mont Saint Michel, running high over the rocky coast, and it offers wonderful views of

Cancale Bay and Dol Marshes. Long ago, at the time of the Celts and the Druids, it was, like Mont Saint Michel itself, a sacred place. The first castle Richeux was built around 1030 by Richer, a nobleman. The castle was attacked by pirates and the Normans, and later stimm, it was destroyed by the army of Henry IV. In the beginning of the 17th century, a fort was built on this strategic spot, but after several attacks, it was taken by the English. In the 1920s, 'Madame Shaki' appeared on the scene. She bought the grounds which bordered the dyke and the rocky coast. In 1925, she had this magnificent fairytale villa and its wonderful French gardens built. But the Second World War destroyed the peace and quiet and the German Kommandatur claimed the house during the occupation. In May 1922 we bought the estate, renovated it and landscaped the park. This extension of 'Maison de Bricourt' came from an ongoing desire to help our clients enjoy the bay of Mont Saint Michel in all its magic."

Jane and Olivier Roellinger.

Le Mont-Blanc

-If there is one hotel in the Alps that is worthy of bearing the name of this high and majestic mountain, it is this hotel in Megève, a trendy, but also typical mountain village in the French Savoy region. In 1949, when winter sports were a new phenomenon, this gorgeous chalet was completely refurbished to receive the French jet-set of the time. In trendy Paris circles, skiing, sledging and skating were the rage, the ultimate new experience, and the Hotel 'Le Mont-Blanc' offered high society the comfort, atmosphere, cosiness ands discretion they were used to. Cocteau even called the hotel 'the 21st Paris arrondissement'! Vadim made his film 'Les Liaisons Dangereuses' there and Aznavour, Prince Aly Kahn, François Mitterand, Rita Hayworth and Gilbert Bécaud are among a string of famous visitors.

Over the years, a host of celebrities came to stay. Half a century later, Jocelyne en Jean-Louis Sibuet, who already owned various bijou hotels in Megève and surroundings, decided to renovate this wonderful chalet, whilst keeping its soul intact. In this unique atmosphere, where British influences mix happily with Austrian and Savoyard touches, a great deal of attention has been paid to detail. And when an old English piece of furniture whispers something in Shakespeare's language, another one immediately reminds us that we are in the middle of the Alp meadows.

Some people call 'Le Mont Blanc' a tour de force, others call it magic - magic in the beautiful village of Megève, the most perfect of settings for something as luxurious and elegant as Hotel Le Mont-Blanc.

Montalembert

This fine hotel is situated on the Rive Gauche in the heart of Paris, an area famous for its literature, art, creativity and its long history. The name Montalembert is taken from the street where the hotel is located, and the Count of Montalembert. The latter was a political figure in Paris, but also a publisher: he launched two newspapers, 'l'Avenir' and 'Le Correspondant'. In 1850, he became a member of the famous Académie Française. Hôtel Montalembert was built in 1926 by the architect A. Couard, and has now been completely renovated. The work took ten months, and as a result, this is not only one of the most beautiful luxury hotels in Paris, but also one of the most special. Under the guidance of the hotel group GLA International, interior decorator Christian Liaigre has given the hotel a typical 'Rive Gauche' touch, a combination of originality and classicism in its most pure form. Everything oozes peace and discretion, from the refined details to the materials used for the furniture. In the lounge, the strict, pure lines are in beautiful contrast with the rare antiques. In the café-bar with its contemporary interior, food is served that is a combination of new values and traditional good taste. From the lobby to the restaurant, the large, arched windows, through which a softly filtered light comes in, remind one of the architecture of the thirties. Artificial, movable lighting accentuates the unique interior. And behind glass screens lies a large open room with a wonderful fireplace: the library, where you can imagine that you are in one of the former *'Cafés littéraires'* on the Rive Gauche...

The rooms show a similar exquisite taste: some have a Zen-like, contemporary atmosphere, others have the olde worlde charm of a luxury hotel room in Louis Philippe style, decorated with authentic old furniture from the original Montalembert hotel, beautifully restored by able craftsmen.

Le Yaca

Deep in the heart of Saint-Tropez, in one of its many narrow and romantic alleyways, Le Yaca receives its guests with a great deal of friendly intimacy. The old house has kept its 18th-century charm beautifully. The walls of the small fisherman's houses are covered in climbing plants, and exude a friendly homeliness. When Le Yaca was built in 1722, it was a typical village house with a shaded courtyard, such as can be found in many of the streets of Saint-Tropez. Who could have

imagined that less than two centuries later, the house would become a meeting place for impressionist painters such as Paul Signac, Matisse, and Dunoyer de Segonzac? Each of them had their own whims, but all of them felt very much at home there.

After the second World War, Philippe Tallien, a former dancer with the Ballet of Monte Carlo and an antiquarian, fell for the charms of the house: he bought it, redecorated it and made it into an hotel which he called l'Aïoli. Thank to the *savoir vivre* of the owner, who was the heart and soul of the restaurant and bar, the hotel became very popular from 1950 onwards. This was the place in Saint-Tropez where people came to see and to be seen.

Orson Welles was one regular visitor; he often stayed more than two months at a time. He would order his favourite dishes and prepare them himself, alongside the chef!

In 1968, l'Aïoli was renamed Le Yaca. The hotel has now been completely renovated and the patio now boasts a magnificent swimming pool. In 1980, Jacques

Huret became its new owner and after further improvements, the hotel obtained four stars. The vast majority of the rooms and suites have a panoramic view of Saint-Tropez bay. But the rooms with a view of the citadel or the old town are no less charming.

At night, it is a treat to sit and enjoy the fresh air and peacefulness of the courtyard by the pool, where you can taste real Italian *haute cuisine*. Unless you prefer to eat in the elegant surroundings of L'Arlequin restaurant... wonderful in every sense.

Saint-Tropez would not be the same without its picturesque little harbour and countless luxury yachts. And to give its guests a real taste of the local atmosphere, Le Yaca offers them the opportunity to hire the hotel's private yacht, including the crew - a unique experience indeed.

Château de Curzay

Before the Marchioness de l'Hôpital started to build the first parts of the current castle in 1700, the estate had already had a colourful history, harking back to the Middle Ages.

The Marchioness was a widow, but she was a very active and ambitious woman for her times. She ran and developed the entire estate herself, laying the foundations for the current castle and its estate. Seven generations, all of them good fathers and husbands, followed each other, until the death of Elie de Curzay in 1939. In 1940 the castle became a refuge

for the Belgian royal family who had fled the war, but soon after that, it was confiscated by the German troops.

Thanks to Colonel L'Hotte, whose wife inherited the estate, the castle was restored to its former glory. Now, the Château de Curzay is a magnificent Relais & Châteaux hotel, with 22 guest rooms, which have names such as Mathilde, Marie and Josephine, and glorious reception rooms such as the 'Salle de Chasse', where breakfast is served, the 'Salon de Musique' and the 'Salon du Vicomte', which all exude a wonderful 18th century atmosphere.

The castle is surrounded by 120 hectares of parkland, with the river Vonne flowing through it. It is wonderful to stroll down the stately, tree-shadowed lanes, admiring the two hundred year-old cedars, or sit on the terrace by the swimming pool beneath the shade of the 12th century turrets.

This is a wonderful place for horse riding, and the estate possesses no less than 28 stables. The environment offers culture, nature and a long history, but also cutting edge technology, for nearby is the well-known Futuroscope, where the most advanced three-dimensional image technology immerses the visitor in the wonderful world of Atlantis, Cyberworld and the curious depths of the ocean. Talk about contrasts!

L'Hostellerie de l'Abbaye de la Celle

The village of Celle, near Brignoles, capital of Var, has retained the typical character of a slumbering Provençal area, with its little plantain-bordered square, its old communal wash-house, its fountain, pétanque area and its fascinating narrow streets. This little piece of paradise lives to the rhythm of the wine harvest and the tolling of the bells in the 17th century abbey. This Roman Benedictine monastery, which became a protected building as early as 1886, was closed in the 17th century due to the libertine ways of its young monks.

These days, the Hostellerie de l'Abbaye de la Celle consists of several buildings. The main house was founded in the 17th century. It is a Provençal mansion which was purchased by Madame Fournier, owner of the isle of Porquerolles off the Côte d'Azur coast. In the 1930s she was already running it as an hotel. There are still some guest rooms in the house now, as well as a pâtisserie, the dining room and the kitchens, run by Benoît Witz. His authentic, traditional dishes make use of the best produce and ingredients from local markets and vegetables from the hotel's own extensive gardens. In the historic abbey itself, the immense renovated Benedictine hall now welcomes parties and conventions.

Five new rooms, three of them duplexes with private gardens, look out onto the vineyard of the 'Maison des Vins de Côteaux Varois'. Here, new wine varieties are produced. It is wonderful to stroll in the vast park that surrounds the hotel, with its plantains, chestnut trees, majestic 200-year old cypresses, its vegetable garden, orchards and swimming pool. Each of the ten rooms is named after a herb in the garden or after one of the people who played a role in the history of the estate: eucalyptus, Marie-Antoinette, General De Gaulle... It was in 1997 that Alain Ducasse and his friend Bruno Clément set to work and gave Madame Fournier's hotel a new lease of life.

Hostellerie de l'Abbaye de la Celle has been restored and renovated with the invaluable help of many clever local craftsmen, supervised by Brignoles architect Robert Michel. Thus, the hotel has started a new life, but without losing the timeless atmosphere of long ago.

La Maison Troisgros

Discover the wealth and variety of this unique area, nestling between Auverge, the Bourbonnais, Lyon and Bourgogne, and take Roanne as your starting point, for that is where you will find one of the best hotel-restaurants in all of France.

In 1930 Jean-Baptiste and Marie Troisgros became owners of 'Hôtel de Platanes' opposite the Roanne station. Later, they renamed it the 'Hôtel Moderne'. Sitting around a huge table, guests enjoyed the wonderful dishes that mother Troisgros cooked, and sipped the beautiful wines provided by Jean-Baptiste. Their sons, Jean and Pierre, were no older than 15 when they started work in the kitchen, and they showed a same fervour and love of good food. Later, they gained experience in Paris and elsewhere in the Provence. Both of them married in 1953 and together they extended the family business under the revised name of 'Hôtel-Restaurant des Frères Troisgros'.

They were soon mentioned in restaurant guides and their favoured star rose swiftly: a first 'macaron' in the Guide Michelin in 1955, a second in 1965 and yet a third in 1968; four 'chef's hats' and 18/20 in Gault Millau and four stars in the Bottin Gourmand. In 1970, they bought the

house next door and extended and modernised the business.
Jean died in 1983 and a new partnership was formed: Pierre and his son Michel, who had gained culinary experience working for Girardet, Taillevent and Guérard.
Michel and his wife Marie-Pierre have created their own atmosphere and ambience in the hotel and restaurant. They are passionately interested in interior design and architecture, and called on the famous Christian Liaigre to restyle their restaurant. The ten rooms, mezzanine, sitting room and lobby were decorated by designer-architect François Champsaut. These days, La Maison Troisgros exudes world class, not only in its cuisine, but also in its wonderful and beguiling interiors.

Ferme Saint-Siméon

"Honfleur has always been the *nec plus ultra* of my dreams", Baudelaire once said. Honfleur, with its picturesque narrow streets and its old houses, at the gates of 'Pays d'Auge' and the 'Flower Coast', is a leisure and fishing harbour. Its old inner harbour, designed by Duquesne and the 'Lieutenance', dates from the 16th century. The Normandy farmhouse Ferme Saint Siméon, built a century later, is closely related to the Impressionist movement. Monet, Sisley, Diaz, Boudin and many other artists met at the 'Auberge de la Mère Toutain', as it was then famously called. Mère Toutain was very generous with the cider, and she inspired the painters, who founded the 'Honfleur School' here, which was the birth of Impressionism. Each room is different, with antique furniture, fine materials and an eye for detail.

The restaurant lies opposite the estuary and offer a delicious, rich Normandy cuisine. The hotel is a real garden of Eden, with large rooms looking out onto the lawns and flower-beds. There is an extensive health suite, where you can relax or enjoy a massage or beauty treatment with natural products, with a pool, sauna, jacuzzi, steam room and fitness room. In the garden, 'La Chaumière' can be found, an annexe once depicted by Monet himself, and which now, in honour of the Honfleur School, offers young artists the opportunity to come and paint here.

The coast where the Allies landed during World war II is only half an hour's drive from the hotel and then, of course, there is Mont Saint-Michel, the most visited tourist attraction in France. Also worth visiting is the Seine valley, with its beautiful diffused light, and Monet's Giverny. And if you have some time to spare, don't forget Rouen and its cathedral, the pilgrim's town of Lisieux and the Sainte-Thérèse Basilique, Bayeux with its famous tapestry, Etrétat, the seaside towns of Deauville and Trouville and, of course, don't forget the sea!

Les Deux Abbesses

Saint-Arcons-d'Allier, an ancient hamlet with only twenty inhabitants, is nestled in the heart of the Auvergne. You will find a very special hotel there. It all started in the seventies, when the local mayor decided that Saint-Arcons, which was almost deserted, needed a new lease of life. It took Laurence Perceval and Bernard Massas nearly 25 years to renovate the village, which is like an island in a spot where two rivers come together. These days, it is as if the cobbled streets of the village form the corridors of the hotel. The castle, a IXth century stronghold, houses the reception lobby, the dining room, 'Salon Bleu' and the smoking room. The turrets were added during the Renaissance by abbesses Gabriëlle and Isabeau de la Fayette (hence the name 'Les Deux Abbesses'). The garden and terrace of the castle border on a Roman church, the bells of which strike the passing hours in this peaceful village. In the Mediterranean-like climate, the hotel swimming pool, overlooking the river, offers welcome refreshment to the guests. When you stay here, you have a difficult choice to make between the small houses, 'La Maison du Notaire', 'La Maison Carabo' and 'La Maison Coupé', the rooms in the old stables or the 'Maison des Bessons'.

There is no better way to start the day than with a generous rural breakfast of croissants, home-made jam, yoghurt and fresh fruit. Later, the chef will pick vegetables and herbs in the 'Jardin des Simples', with which he will prepare a delicious and adventurous evening meal. That evening, a few music notes will tell you that dinner is ready, so it is time to leave the garden where you have been enjoying your pre-dinner drink, and to sit down to a meal by candlelight that has all the wonderful flavours of the region.

The next day, there is plenty of time to do absolutely nothing but enjoy the beautiful surroundings. Or if you want to, there is a variety of sporting activities: mountain-biking riding, canoeing or just simply walking or visiting the Auvergne with its fascinating castles, abbeys and Roman churches.

Château de Locguénolé

An old legend tells that Saint Guénolé, chased by the devil, crossed the estuary in the south of Brittany in one giant step, and set up residence in the area that now houses the castle, which, from then on, has been called Locguénolé or 'the place of Saint Guénolé'. The castle as it is now, dates from the beginning of the 19th century. But its history goes back much further. According to old legal papers, the family tree of the current owners can be traced to the 16th century. First, Locguénolé was owned by the Marquess of Latour-Maubourg, then by the Count de Perrien and now by the family de la Sablière.

The estate adjoining the castle dates from the 18th century. The current castle was renovated in 1810, and stands in the middle of magnificent parklands, designed by André de Versailles, one of the best French landscape gardeners. Opposite the castle there are small houses with walled-in gardens. In 1968, the castle was made into an hotel by the de la Sablière family. By using the premises for commercial purposes, they could safeguard their inheritance. Locguénolé became one of the first Relais & Châteaux hotels in Brittany.

It is furnished with 18th century antiques and it has 18 rooms and 4 suites. The restaurant was awarded 17 out of 20 by Gault Millau 2000, a fine example of the rich Breton tradition of superior gastronomy! There is a jetty which allows clients to arrive by sea and to leave for boat trips to the wonderful world of the Breton south coast, with its countless charming little islands, bays, creeks, golden yellow beaches and little fishing harbours.

Le Cagnard

'Le Cagnard' is Provençal for 'the sun shining on every side'. The history of this glorious estate is directly linked with the medieval fortress here. The house, like the fortress, dates far back to the 14th century. The 'Salle des Gardes' with its vaults, its fireplace and subterranean corridor leading to the castle, bears witness to this long history. From the beginning of the last century, the building was an inn. In 1925, the portrait painter Emile Wery painted the medieval vaulted ceilings, adding an exotic touch. Through the ages, Le Cagnard has been visitied by a host of famous guests. Musketeer d'Artagnan stayed here, and Nicolette and Aucassin lived out their forbidden romance in the house. Aucassin, son of the local landlord, fell in love with Nicolette, who was then kept prisoner in the cellars of the castle. Two rooms in the hotel bear their names... Simone de Beauvoir, Antoine de Saint Exupéry and many famous painters found peace and quiet here.

In 1960 the Barels fell for the charms of this old inn, and transformed it into a luxury hotel. Several years ago their daughter Mrs. Laroche, and her husband took over and continued the family tradition. In 1974, Le Cagnard became part of Relais & Châteaux.
There are eight rooms in the main building, another 17 rooms can be found in adjoining houses in the village. The ceiling of the restaurant is divided into nearly 200 hand-painted panels, and draw the eye up to the azure-blue sky.
Le Cagnard has a wonderful Michelin-starred restaurant, where chef Jean-Yves Johanny rules. The hotel can be found in the heart of the Côte d'Azur, in the village of Haut-de-Cagnes, a romantic beauty spot. Guests can enjoy the miles of beautiful coastline with its beaches and water sports, or go inland and discover lovely, romantic villages such as Eze or Saint-Paul de Vence, or they can go trekking, canyoning or discover the nature reserve of Mercantour.

La Verniaz et ses Chalets

'La Verniaz', an old farmhouse in typical Savoy style, situated between Lake Geneva and the Alps, owes its name to the spring that provides Evian with its healing waters.

In 1920, the farm was transformed into an hotel by a certain Auguste Florettini, a Swiss from the Grisons area, who had been a major domus of the Russian Czar in St. Petersburg. It is from that time that 'La Potinière d'Evian' dates, a tearoom where people came to eat cakes and waffles in the shade of chestnut trees. By request of his customers, 'Florio' installed some rooms in the stables, in what is now the 'Closerie'. Later, the old corn shed was transformed into guest accommodation and became 'Le Chalet du Coq Hardi'. Soon, La Verniaz was bursting at the seams. Often, there were no more than two important guests, but they brought their entourage along with them; Prince Louis II of Monaco among them, and François Coty, the super-rich perfume king. The fact that chef Alexis Sipiagune, who had followed Florettini from Russia, was such a superior cook, was certainly an added attraction.

Nowadays, La Verniaz is managed by Suzanne and Marcel Verdier, the current owners, and it has become a typical Savoyard hamlet, consisting of old houses, chalets that have been beautifully integrated into a park full of magnificent trees, lawns, sunny terraces and fountains. The rooms with their balconies are spacious, beautifully furnished and decorated with fresh wild flowers. The restaurant has an open fire where meat and freshly-caught fish are prepared in front of the guests. The chef produces a wonderful fresh cuisine with dishes such as *Féra du lac cuite sur la peau, sauce au vermouth*, or *volaille de Bresse entière à la broche*, and *tarte chaude aux pommes et glace au miel de Savoie*.

Suzanne and Marcel can offer their guests a unique combination: seventy years of exquisite French-Swiss hospitality and superior cuisine, with a Russian soul and a British country club touch.

La Maison Blanche

Place des Lices in Saint-Tropez is exactly the kind of place you imagine when you think of a traditional French square: age old plantains shield the locals from the sun while they play *jeu de boules* on the well-trodden soil; there are typical cafes with terraces everywhere, and stylishly-dressed waiters who, with a flourish pour their customers a *pastis* or a *kir*, filling their glasses to the very brim. The square is surrounded by grand houses where notables once lived. The most special, the most exciting and probably the largest of all is a white house with a beautiful garden, which at the beginning of the 20th century was know as "La Maison du Docteur" - the doctor's house. Today, its beautiful façade hides the first design hotel in Saint-Tropez. Bénédicte and Gilles Noubel are the proud owners of this hotel with its wonderful architecture and superior interior design. They engaged Fabienne Villacrèces, an interior designer from Carcassonne, to create this gem, and it was the first hotel Fabienne ever took in hand. Once you enter the door, you step into a wondrous world of design, filled with squares and the letters "MB", for Maison Blanche.

The outside of the house was kept in its authentic state, but everything has been painted a brilliant white, which enhances the architectural beauty of the building. The garden is magnificent: a large terrace built in exotic hazrdwood covers most of the grounds, and two large parasol pines cast their long, much-needed shadows. The terrace, which also has a summer bar, is surrounded by bamboo, jasmine and palm trees. It is a wonderful place to have breakfast and to watch the *"va et vient"* of the locals, the celebrities and the would-be celebrities that go by on the Place des Lices.

Le Lodge Parc

In the shadow of the Mont Blanc, nestling between Alpine meadows, lies the beautiful mountain village of Megève. It has an authentic, medieval charm, beautiful boutiques and wonderful narrow streets where horse-drawn carriages go by. Megère has real French style and *joie de vivre*, and is well known for its *après-ski*. When they started the 'Companie des Hôtels de Montagne', Jocelyne and Jean-Louis Sibuet decided to bring their different Megève hotels under one banner: Les Fermes de Marie, Le Mont Blanc, Le Coin du Feu, Les Fermes de Grand Champs and the latest: Le Lodge Parc.

At a stone's throw from the ski lifts, surrounded by green parkland in the middle of the old village, Le Lodge Parc, formerly known as Grand-Hôtel du Parc, has a very privileged location. When you enter, you immediately feel the charm of the cosy, unique decoration: everything is in natural wood, with stone fireplaces, tartan materials and old leather. There is a large collection of objects and souvenirs from all over the world: an airplane propellor,

a sculpted bear, antique wooden skis, fishing tackle from long ago, old hunting trophies... each telling their own story about people and their passions.

The rooms are exquisite and there is a bar with a fishing theme. When it comes to the cuisine, the menu *'Découverte de Saveurs du Monde'* offers you tastes from all over the world. Jocelyne and Jean-Louis Sibuet have taken up the challenge and won: they wanted to give their guests the feeling that they were staying in a lodge on the banks of a lake in the American Adirondacks at the time of the gold rush! And in order to meet the demands of people who associate holiday with sport, Le Lodge Parc has set up a *Comptoir des Sports et des Excursions*. Amongst the many activities on offer, the ski safari on Mont Blanc is especially recommended. A route which allows the more adventurous skiers to discover, under expert guidance, the most beautiful pistes of Megève, Chamonix, Saint Gervais and Courmayeur.

Domaine des Hauts de Loire

Slowly, the stately River Loire flows through the heart of France, like a king sauntering through his palace, flanked by rows of curtsying subjects, self-assured, and well aware of his dignity. To the left and right, wonderful estates, parks, castles, historic towns and cities glide by. If you stay on the banks of this elegant river, in this superbly historic area, it would be a pity not to stay in the kind of accommodation worthy of the surroundings.
At the Domaine des Hauts de Loire, with its conveniently a central position amongst the most important castles, between the towns of Blois and Tours, you cannot help but fall under the charming spell of the area. The old 19th century hunting lodge (built by the Count of Rostaing on a spot where once a medieval fortress rose up) has retained all of its original glory. It is surrounded by a beautiful park, with a pond on which elegant swans float, and long, shady lanes that invite you to take endless walks.

The exquisite rooms and apartments are divided between the castle itself and the mansion next door, built in the style of the region.
The Bonnival family, the current owners and managers, ensure the cuisine and the wonderful Loire wines are of the same superior level as the accommodation. You could hardly stay anywhere more central. The historic towns of Blois and Tours are close by, the castles of Amboise, Chambord, Cheverny and Chaumont surround the estate like a wonderful garland. A special tip to make your stay here even more regal: go on a helicopter trip, organised by the hotel, or board a balloon and float high over all the beautiful castles and towns. And don't forget to admire the stately Loire, which flows like a silver ribbon through the landscape... Slow and dignified.

Le Club de Cavalière

It is 9 o'clock in the morning and I am sitting on the terrace outside my room, a breakfast of succulent croissants, fresh baguette and hot café-crème before me. The rising sun colours the brightening waters of the Mediterranean as I watch. Yachts the size of cruise ships glide across glittering waves between the coast of Le Lavendou and the islands of Port Cros and Porquerolles. Beneath me, on the terrace of the restaurant where breakfast is being served, I can hear the carefree laughter of happy holiday makers.

Yesterday I spent hours there, enjoying a long and leisurely dinner. It was one of the most perfect evenings I have ever experienced. The open-air restaurant is separated from the sea only by a stretch of soft, white beach. And the glittering sea, in which the moon was reflected, made a calm, soothing sounds as I enjoyed a number of exquisite dishes from the 'Carte Grill'.

But now, on my terrace, I'm studying a travel guide on the Côte d'Azur, today, I want to discover the area. Beautiful Saint-Tropez is nearby, the Var mountains with their Provençal villages rise up behind the hotel and on the coast are the Hyères islands.

Some good advice: one really must go to the nearby isle of Giens, and take the ferry to the little, peaceful Ile de Porquerolles. It won't take more than 20 minutes. Rent a bicycle (there are no cars on the island) and discover this beautiful area with its deep blue bays, its maquis and its very tropical village square. It feels, indeed, like Africa!

La Bastide de Marie

A small hotel? A guest house? In fact, this is neither. It would be better to call it an estate where one can spend a few hours or days, letting the time tick slowly by, sipping a glass of wine in an exquisite and peaceful environment.

On the terrace, in the shade of a large lime-tree, the Provence whispers in your ear that life is different here than at home. The scents and the colours are an invitation to cultivate a delightful sense of 'dolce far niente'. And what can be more delightful than to play a game of pétanque in the evening, in the fresh air, building up an appetite for yet another culinary adventure based on olive oil.

The next day, you will no doubt fall under the spell of Menerbes, one of the typical villages in the surroundings, or the nature reserve of Lubéron. Every day, little local markets welcome you with their regional produce, bathed in the scents and heady

colours of the Provence. The antique market of Isle sur la Sorgue is a perfect meeting place for antique lovers. Gordes, impregnated with Provençal charm, is known for its castle housing Pol Mara's museum, the village of Les Bories is famous for its unique 17th-century stone shepherds' houses, and Roussillon has its red rocks, sand and earth. You are spoiled for choice... and leaving will not be easy!

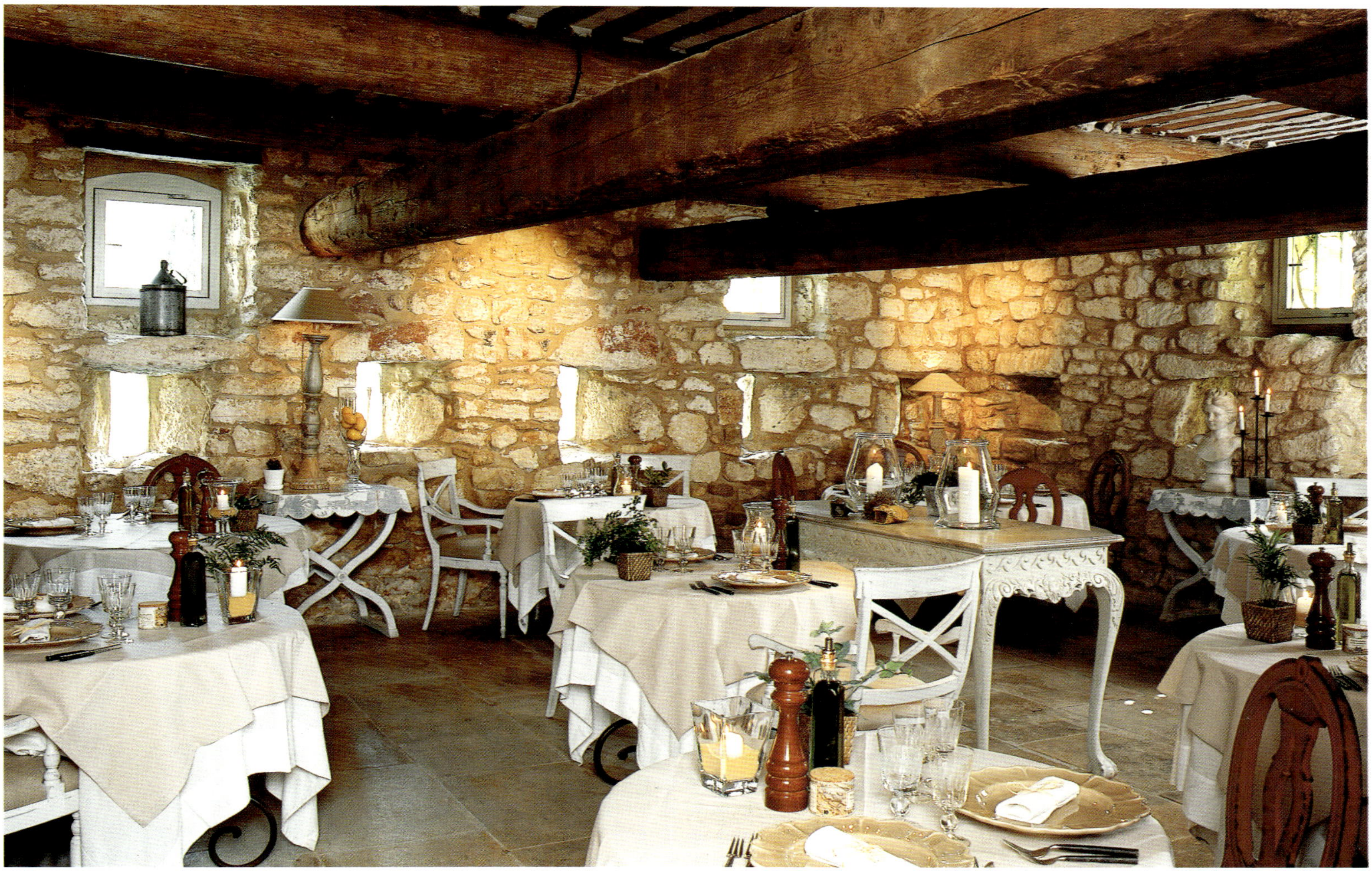

DOMAINE DE MARIE
2000
BASTIDE DE MARIE
2000
DOMAINE DE MARIE
2000
BASTIDE DE MARIE

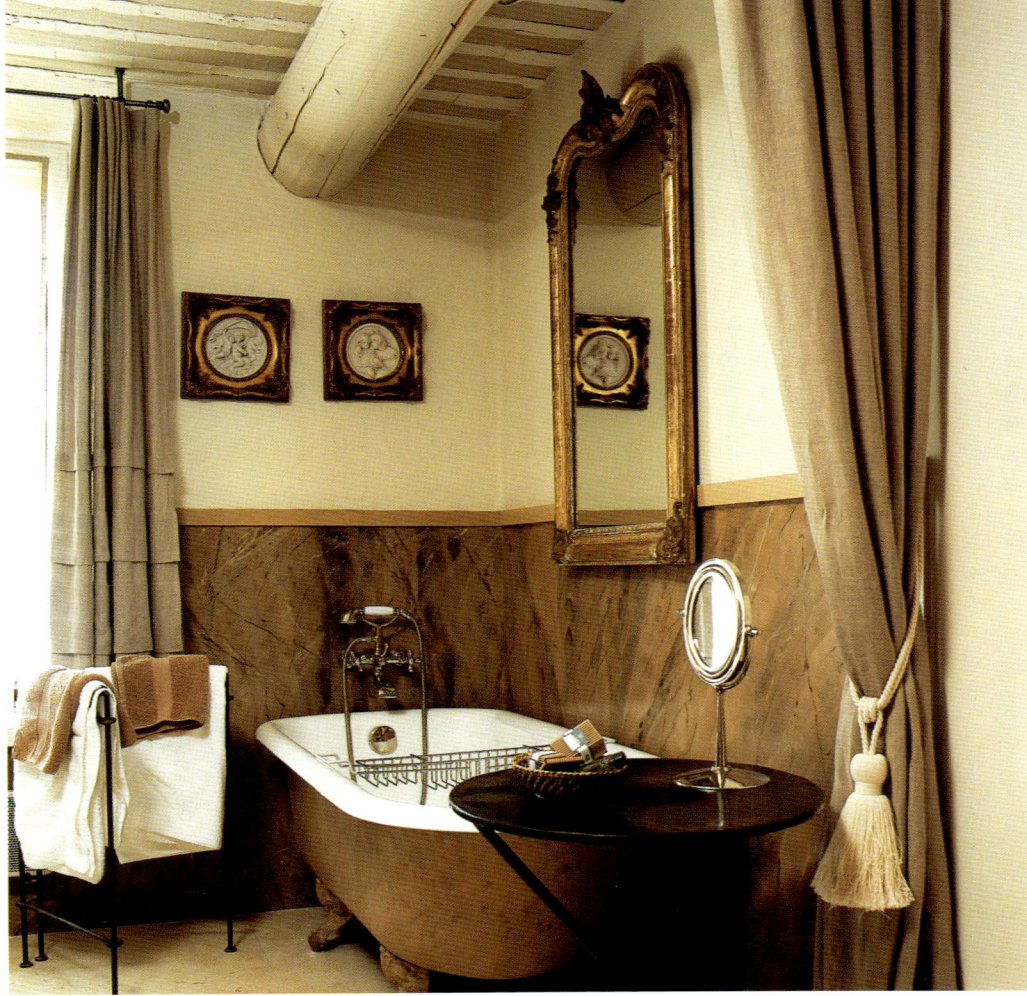

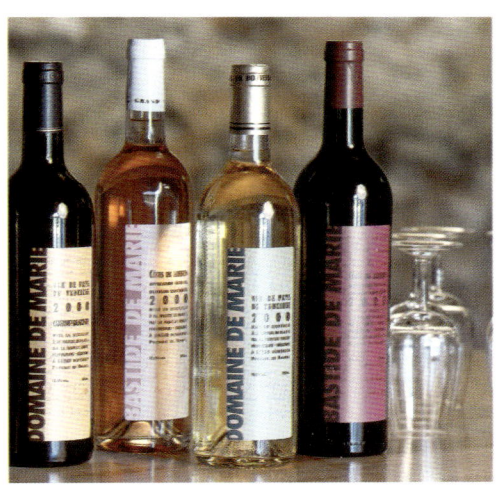

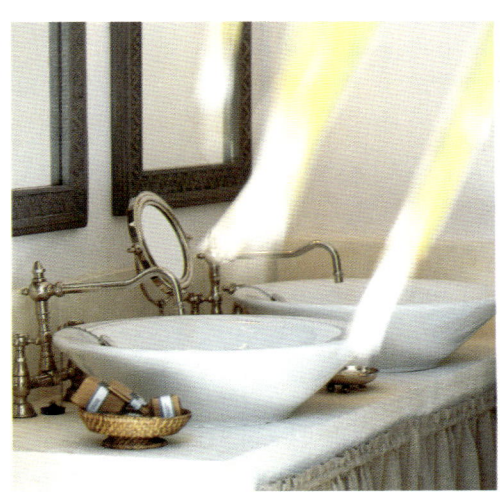

Cour des Loges

In Vieux Lyon, the medieval part of the city of Lyon, which has been classed as a world heritage area by UNESCO, stand four houses that together form the hotel Cour des Loges. It has obvious Italian influences, due to the fact that Lyon had (and still has) a considerable Italian community, and the passion the French kings had for everything Italian. These buildings were built during the Renaissance for the many tradesmen, bankers and printers in Lyon, a city which was then extremely wealthy thanks to its tax-free trading status. The king and his courtiers would often come to stay. Later,

Claude de Beaumont, Master of Burgundy, bought the houses for his own use... and then left them to the Jesuit monks, who stayed there until their possessions were confiscated during the French revolution. Then, the houses were rented out by the locals. Just like in the fairytale of Sleeping Beauty, Vieux Lyon - and the four houses themselves - were forgotten for a many years, and it wasn't until the second half of the 1970s that they awoke, after years of neglect.
Renovation work started in 1981 and took five years. But more even than the long history of this part of town, where every brick tells a story, it is the combination of different eras and styles that makes Cour de Loges so unique. It is a subtly harmonious blend of the spirit of the Renaissance with con-

temporary design. Greeat care has been taken to preserve the magical charm of the interior decor, whilst providing the highest standards of modern comfort for the guests. The Cour des Loges is unique... and uniquely satisfying.

Les Sources de Caudalie

This is an unpublished fairytale. On my search for the most beautiful hotels in the world, I have never seen anything like it. No other place has so creatively made use of the natural elements, of all the beauty and good things Mother Nature provides the inhabitants of the world in certain particularly favoured places.

It all started in 1990, when Florence and Daniel Cathiard left the hectic city of Paris and set aside their brilliant careers to find a new challenge in life. And what a challenge it was! They bought the famous, exclusive vineyards of 'Smith Haut Lafitte', a stone's throw from the city of Bordeaux and the Bay of Arcachon. But that was not all: during the wine harvest in 1993 their daughter Mathilde, together with a small team of therapy lecturers in Bordeaux, developed 'vinotherapy', a therapy based on wine extracts. This health and anti-ageing tratment has proved enormously succesful. But Mother Nature bestowed even more blessings on them: on the premises was a hot water spring, rich in iron, sulphur and fluor, and the waters were integrated in the therapy. Thus, the concept of 'Sources de Caudalie' was born: in the midst of a noble vineyard, a health spa and a unique, luxurious hotel complex were built.

121

The architecture and the 39 rooms and suites in the various buildings bear testimony to the creativity of the owners: 'La Bastide des Grands Crus', 'Le Comptoir des Indes', a charming pile-dwelling in the lake, 'La Cabane Tchanquée' and 'l'Ile aux Oiseaux'… each room is furnished differently and has its own tale to tell. The two restaurants are headed by star-awarded chef Didier Banyols and his wife Marie-Louise, a renowned wine specialist, selected ten thousand of the finest wines for the hotel's immense wine cellar. This is France at its very best!

Hôtel d'Europe

Hôtel d'Europe can be found in one of the most beautiful and oldest mansions that nobility has ever owned in the papal city of Avignon. The first coats of arms that decorated its walls were those of Amat de Graveson (1580), but the most famous of these noble families was that of Marguerite de Crillon, after whom the grand square was named that stretches from the hotel to the Porte de l'Oulle.

In 1799, the house was bought by the widow Madame Pierron. Since then, many illustrious travellers from the worlds of politics, business and religion have stayed at Hôtel d'Europe. Among the first was Napoléon Bonaparte himself. Haunted by the Directoire regime, Bonaparte came hid himself in the hotel for a crucial few days. On his way to join his army in Italy, he called in again, and it is from that occasion that the following anecdote dates: he treated all his officers to dinner and made sure that he thanked Madame Pierron for the wonderful meal, but because he knew that his Treasurer was a real glutton, he added: "Madame, if you normally charge 25 francs for your meal, you should ask for 30 francs in this case!"

These days, friendliness and hospitality are still two of the greatest assets at Hôtel d'Europe. It is still a very special home away from home within the ancient walls of Avignon, a stopping place in the heart of the Provence. After Napoléon, it is now your turn.

Le Domaine des Hautes Roches

It is amongst these carved-out rocks, the stone of which was used to build the magnificent castles of the Loire that, after one and a half years of building and renovation works, the Domaine des Hautes Roches opened its door as a hotel in 1989. It was the passion of one man, Philippe Mollard, which saved the caves and the 18th-century Pavilion. Before the complex became the first troglodyte hotel in France, the rooms were used by the monks of the nearby Marmoutier Abbey, and were a refuge during the religious wars. Later, mushrooms were grown in the caves and the 'Vin Lanternois', which became famous through the writings of Rabelais, was laid to mature here. For more than a century, from 1855 to 1975, the Domaine des Pentes was regarded as one of the best 'Vouvray' wine houses, after which it became a storage place for brandy. Finally it lay deserted, covered in the greenery that grows so abundantly in this climate on the banks of the river Loire. Today, the hotel has fifteen luxurious rooms, twelve of which are situated actually within the caves, and three more classic rooms in the pavilion. Claustrophobics need not worry that they will feel trapped here: all rooms have large windows looking out on the Loire, on one of the rare spots of the river where the view is unimpaired. The bar has also been built in a cave, in what once was the abbey kitchens. The monumental fireplace and the bread oven can still be seen. It is a wonderful experience to sit here drinking an aperitif, and then to go to the restaurant in the villa on the river. Even better: as soon as weather permits, chef Didier Edon serves his creations outside under the lime trees.

135

Royal Rivièra

The former fishing harbour of Saint-Jean-Cap Ferrat is now an exclusive holiday resort, known for its peace and quiet. 'Le Cap', on the far south, gave its name to the entire peninsula, which stretches from Villefranche to the bay of Fourmis near Beaulieu. In a prime position, at the foot of Cap Ferrat, stands the Hotel Royal Rivièra, which was built in 1905 and today is a favourite with the Rivièra's rich and cosmopolitan clientele, who often spend entire winters here. The monumental reception rooms and immense rooms with their wonderful sea views make this a unique place to stay. Famous names from the film and music world, and many distuinguished artists have contributed to the fame of the Royal Rivièra. The hotel is surrounded by a park with a large swimming pool, and it is uniquely located right on the Mediterranean coast. The casino of Beaulieu and the museum Ephrussi de Rothschild and the Villa Kérylos are less than a stone's throw away.

The 77 rooms and suites, divided over four floors, offer all possible modern comforts. The restaurants combine gastronomy with a refined *joie de vivre*: 'Le Panorama' has wonderful sea views, 'La Pergola', near the pool, offers wonderful buffet meals and 'La Terrasse' is an ideal spot to enjoy breakfast in the morning sun, or to dine as the sun is setting, by the sound of the waves.

Hôtel Lancaster

The Prince and Princess de Hennin, regulars at the Royal Court, once live on the Champs Elysées in a magnificent *hôtel particulier*, surrounded by extensive parklands. Part of these were sold off to Monsieur Drake del Castillo. He built a mansion there with four floors, each containing a separate apartment, in a style that was very avant-garde at the time: the Haussmann style. In 1925, Swiss hotelier Emile Wolf bought the house, and made it into a luxury hotel, in the style of the swinging twenties and thirties. Emile Wolf happily took advantage of the fact that the manageress of Hôtel Lancaster was the daughter of a Paris antique dealer, and furnished the rooms and salons with precious furniture and works of art, which even now greatly contribute to the reputation of the hotel. The many collector's items lend a sophisticated and intimate touch: everywhere you will find 18th century furniture, paintings, lamps, Baccarat crystal, carpets and china.

145

In 1970 Monsieur Wolf retired from the business and he handed the Hôtel Lancaster over to the renowned Savoy hotel chain. In 1995 the hotel was bought by a group of private investors and its management put in the hands of GLA International, an organisation which specialises in running luxury hotels. The new manageress, Madame Grace Leo Andrieu instigated important renovation works, trying to add a touch of contemporary decorative art to the original character of the hotel. Extensive research was done to find out what patterns were used in the 18th and 19th centuries for curtains and wall-hangings. No less than 70 different materials were chosen by Braquenié and Pierre Frey, the contemporary furniture was designed by Christian Liaigre and the old furniture was completely renovated by craftsmen. But the essence of the place remains the same: a *hôtel particulier* which combines intimacy and discretion with luxury and beauty.

Les Muscadins

Although Mougins is only a stone's throw from the cosy, but often hectically busy town of Cannes, it really feels as if you are in the middle of the Provence, where life is slow and peaceful. From high on its hill, the medieval village looks happily down on the busy comings and goings at its feet, at the luxury yachts that arrive and depart from the many small harbours and the azure blue waters sparkling between the little islands of Lérins. It was Picasso himself who discovered Mougins in 1935 and since then, the *beau monde* from Cannes mingle with the locals, who take in their glamour with equanimity.

On the terraces of the Place de la Mairie there are more important things to consider: a glass of pastis or rosé, or the pétanque game of the *habitués*... Yet, there once was a time when this little village was more important than Cannes! Long before Picasso came here to admire the view, some time at the beginning of the century, at the outskirts of the village, there was a small hotel with the name 'Fixed Horizon'. It was nothing special: there were just a few rooms for travellers, but the name was spot on: the view over the perfume city of Grasse and the hinterland, the coast, the islands and the bay was out of this world. There, on that same exquisite spot, now stands an hotel that is one of the very best in the south of France. The man behind this wonderful creation is Eddy Bianchini, an Italian American. What makes the interior of this hotel so unique, is that he has managed to combine seven styles and historic periods in a harmonious and original way; The cuisine is equally creative: Eddy Bianchini was the only American to gain a Michelin star in 1991. When he arrived here in 1982, he exclaimed: *'This is heaven! There is no reason to die now...'* Which says a lot about the man and the hotel.

Bernard Loiseau
La Côte d'Or

Bernard Loiseau is a something of a phenomenon in France. His culinary philosophy is to use as little sugar and fat as possible and retain the original flavours of the local produce. Thus, he has managed to let a fresh wind blow through French cuisine. His restaurant justly gained the highest praise in various gastronomic guides, including three Michelin stars. In the 18th century, La Côte d'Or was a coaching inn and in the sixties and seventies, it was made famous by the culinary art of chef Alexandre Dumaine. At the time, 'La Côte d'Or' in Saulieu, 'Point' in Vienne and 'Pic' in Valence were the three cuilinary highlights on the axis connecting Paris with the distant Mediterranean.

The four-star hotel, which looks onto a traditional English garden, has 32 rooms, most of which have their own terrace or balcony. They have been finished in Burgundy stone and old wood, have all mod cons and exude the atmosphere of the area. There is a generous wine cellar, where guests can taste the wines -many of them from Burgundy- and the former hotel bar now has a shop, where you can buy herbs, wines, liqueurs - indeed, everything you might need for the table. All these products can also be bought on the internet (www.shop.bernard-loiseau.com). The name of hotel-restaurant 'La Côte d'Or' refers to the magic hills between Beaune and Dijon, a real mecca of wine châteaux and vineyards of Burgundy.

Le Pigonnet

Aix,

The fresh clatter of fountains,
but also, two steps from hectic city life,
a few minutes from the noble façades,
the statues, the squares,
the artistic gardens and the atmosphere
of the bastides.
When Paul Cézanne placed his easel
here, charm already was everywhere,
and it still is.
Larger, and even more beautiful than
before, the mansion is now an hotel.
Since 1924, one and the same family has
been receiving you here.
And the decor tells as many stories as the
legendary hospitality.
Impossible not to fall under thee spell of
this large, refined house,
in all its beauty and liveliness.
And instinctively you feel that all modern
comforts arre effortlessly combined
with the souvenirs and precious ancient
objects

This, in a few words, describes this wonderful place. My brother and I grew up and have inherited more than a house from our parents and grandparents. Our parents, who did not come from the Provence, but from the north and the Corrèze region, were immediately seduced by this bastide, then owned by a certain Monsieur de Pigon –hence the name 'Pigonnet'. Many celebrities have spent the night here, such as Président Chirac and Berlusconi, Ronaldo, Alain Delon, Julien Clerc, Clint Eastwood and Princess Caroline of Monaco. One of our associates always greets new arrivals with this amusing little phrase: 'Madame, Monsieur, welcome! This home is yours…'. And then, after a pause, he adds : 'until you leave !'

Gilles Swellen

Grand-Hôtel des Bains

At the time I was writing the book 'Hidden Gems of Provence', I met some fellow countrymen who had left Belgium and opened homes in France where they receive guests from all over the world. Many Belgians seem to have a great affinity with the atmosphere and mentality of their more southerly neighbours: the Grand-Hôtel des Bains, for example, in Locquirec, on the north coast of Brittany, is a real gem. Dominique van Lier and Patricia Matthieu de Wynendaele fell in love with the area and the little coastal village of Locquirec, and they spent many happy times there as tourists, enjoying the peace and quiet, in season and out. They then decided to buy the Grand-Hôtel, set in a magnificent spot on the bay between the 'Côte de Granit Rose' and the 'Côte Sauvage'. The hotel, which was built by Count de Wauthier, is a century old and, over the years, has remained unchanged. It is a real feat that the owners have renovated and embellished the place so considerably, yet have managed to retain the authenticity and the original atmosphere of the building.

Their intention is to attract visitors out of season by welcoming them to a cosy, warm environment. There is nothing better after a long wind-blown walk on the deserted beach, than to dive into the indoor swimming pool of the Grand-Hôtel des Bains, and then to enjoy an aperitif in front of the open fire. After that, it is time for a wonderful meal, prepared by Breton chef Marcel Bourhis. His speciality is a three-course lobster dinner: the first half of the lobster is cooked in the oven with seaweed, then the claws are served *à la nage* with vegetables in Sancerre wine, and the second half of the lobster is grilled at the table in a *corail*-sauce. Before you know it, the clock of the beautiful Saint-Jacques church in Locquirec will be chiming the midnight hour. Back in your room, everything is quiet but the soothing sound of the North Sea waves.

Villa Florentine

What a wonderful way to wake up! You open the curtains of your room and all of Lyon is at your feet: the old city, the peninsula and the Saône and on the horizon… the tips of the Alps! And just as unique as the panorama is the decor of the Villa Florentine: the various floors that follow the movements of the range of hills are filled with a refined luxury worthy of the historical surroundings. When Henry IV married Maria de Medici in 1600 in St. John's Cathedral, Lyon and Florence became closely affiliated. Artists from all over Italy brought the Renaissance to Lyon, and artists from Lyon in their turn came to the Italian peninsula. It was in this fascinating era that the Villa Florentine was built: an Italian villa overlooking the Saône… In 1707 the villa housed a religious congregation, and it was in that year that the "Maison de la Providence" was founded. This institution aimed to give underprivileged city girls a suitable education, so that they would be able to fend for themselves from the age of about twenty. Between 1736 and 1741, a magnificent chapel was added to the building.

Today, it has been beautifully restored and is now the lobby of the hotel. The restaurant "Terrasses de Lyon" offers everything you would expect in this gastronomic world capital. There is also a wonderful wine list, which leans heavily towards the areas around Lyon: Côtes-du-Rhône, Beaujolais and great Bourgogne wines such as Chassagne-Montrachet and Vosne-Romanée.

175

Georges Blanc

It all started before the French Revolution, in the heart of the Bresse, where the Blanc family had been working the land for generations. In 1872, Jean-Louis Blanc and his wife opened an inn in Vonnas. Georges is the fourth generation in the hotel business. In 1962 he finished studying at the hotel school in Thonon-les-Bains. He then went to work in various top restaurants and in 1965 he started in the family business alongside his mother. In 1968, when he was barely twenty-five, he took over from her.

He transformed the modest inn into one of the top names in the 'Relais & Châteaux' hotel chain. Other achievements followed: in 1981 he gained a third star in the Guide Michelin, and Gault Millau awarded him the coveted title of 'Chef of the Year'. This culinary artist, who is at the top of the list in various renowned 'Guides', offers a modern cuisine with fresh produce and a personal touch. He rebuilt the old auberge on the Place du Marché stone by stone. The current 'L'Ancienne Auberge' is a wonderful

replica of his ancestors' restaurant, as it looked in 1900. In the heart of Mâcon, near the old bridge, stands 'Le Saint Laurent', a bistro-style restaurant with a terrace on the banks of the river Saône. It offers regional dishes of the Saône valley. In 1999, the restaurant 'Chez Blanc' opened its doors in Bourg-en-Bresse and the latest addition is 'Le Splendid', in the old town of Lyon.

In spite of the fact that Georges Blanc has one of the best wine cellars in the world, he still wanted to realise an old dream: his own vineyard of 17 hectares in the Mâconnais. Here, excellent wine is produced under the name 'Domaine d'Azenay'.
Both his sons, Fréderic and Alexandre are gripped with the same passion as Georges Blanc. One day, they will take over from him, as family tradition prescribes.

La Riboto de Taven

Riboto de Taven can be found in the 'Vallée de la Fontaine', between Queen Jeanne's Pavilions, a real Renaissance gem, and the entrance to 'Devil's Valley', a wonderful slice of nature that inspired Dante's description of the Inferno in his Divine Comedy. Riboto de Taven is a traditional *mas*, nestling at the foot of the rocks. In 1960, Monsieur and Madame Novi, who had already landscaped the garden using a variety of Mediteranean plants and trees such as cypresses, olives and plane-trees, decided to open a restaurant which, as the years went by, became internationally renowned. Several decades later, their children Christiane and Philippe Theme and Jean-Pierre Novi took over, but the philosophy has remained the same: intimacy, warmth and simplicity. Two 'troglodite', or cave rooms have been constructed, hidden away in the garden behind the terrace, which offers a wonderful view of the old *cité* of Les Baux.

It is hard to imagine that these luxurious, spacious rooms have their roots in down-to-earth rural life: once, olive oil was pressed here. In the summer of 2001, four additional rooms were made to receive an ever-increasing number of guests. They, too, are part of the magic of this very special place.

Useful information

1. **Château de Courcelles**   **page 10**
   8, Rue du Château
   02220 Courcelles-sur-Vesle
   Tel. (33) (0) 3 23 74 13 53
   Fax (33) (0) 3 23 74 06 41
   e-Mail :
   reservation@chateau-de-courcelles.fr
   Website :
   www.chateau-de-courcelles.fr

2. **La Bastide Saint Antoine**   **page 18**
   48, Avenue Henri Dunant
   06130 Grasse
   Tel. (33) (0) 4 93 70 94 94
   Fax (33) (0) 4 93 70 94 95
   e-Mail : info@jacques-chibois.com
   Website : www.jacques-chibois.com

3. **Les Maisons de Bricourt**   **page 22**
   1, rue Duguesclin
   35260 Cancale
   Tel. (33) (0) 2 99 89 64 76
   Fax (33) (0) 2 99 89 88 47
   e-Mail :
   info@maisons-de-bricourt.com
   Website :
   www.maisons-de-bricourt.com

4. **Hôtel Mont Blanc**   **page 28**
   Place de l'Eglise
   74120 Megève
   Tel. (33) (0) 4 50 21 20 02
   Fax (33) (0) 4 50 21 45 28
   e-Mail : contact@c-h-m.com
   Website : www.c-h-m.com

5. **Hôtel Montalembert**   **page 32**
   3, Rue de Montalembert
   75007 Paris
   Tel. (33) (0) 1 45 49 68 68
   Fax (33) (0) 1 45 49 69 49
   e-Mail :
   welcome@hotel-montalembert.fr
   Website : www.montalembert.com

6. **Le Yaca**   **page 38**
   1, Bd d'Aumale
   B.P. 196
   83994 Saint-Tropez
   Tel. (33) (0) 4 94 55 81 00
   Fax (33) (0) 4 94 97 58 50
   e-Mail : hotel-le-yaca@wanadoo.fr
   Website : www.nova.fr/yaca

7. **Château de Curzay**   **page 42**
   86600 Curzay-sur-Vonne
   Tel. (33) (0) 5 49 36 17 00
   Fax (33) (0) 5 49 53 57 69
   e-Mail : curzay@relaischateaux.com
   Website :
   www.relaischateaux.com/curzay

8. **Hostellerie de l'Abbaye de la Celle**   **page 48**
   Place du Général de Gaulle
   83170 La Celle
   Tel. (33) (0) 4 98 05 14 14
   Fax (33) (0) 4 98 05 14 15
   e-Mail : contact@abbaye-celle.com
   Website : www.abbaye-celle.com

9. **La Maison Troisgros**   **page 54**
   Place Jean Troisgros
   42300 Roanne
   Tel. (33) (0) 4 77 71 66 97
   Fax (33) (0) 4 77 70 39 77
   e-Mail : troisgros@avo.fr
   Website : www.troisgros.fr

10. **Ferme Saint Siméon**   **page 58**
    Rue Adolphe-Marais
    14600 Honfleur
    Tel. (33) (0) 2 31 81 78 00
    Fax (33) (0) 2 31 89 48 48
    e-Mail :
    informations@saint-simeon.com
    Website : www.saint-simeon.com

11. **Les Deux Abbesses**   **page 64**
    Le Château
    43300 Saint-Arcons-d'Allier
    Tel. (33) (0) 4 71 74 03 08
    Fax (33) (0) 4 71 74 05 30
    e-Mail :
    direction@les-deux-abbesses.fr
    Website : www.les-deux-abbesses.fr

12. **Château de Locguénolé**   **page 70**
    Route de Port-Louis en Kervignac
    56700 Hennebont
    Tel. (33) (0) 2 97 76 76 76
    Fax (33) (0) 2 97 76 82 35
    e-Mail :
    locguenole@relaischateaux.fr
    Website :
    www.chateau-de-locguenole.fr

13. **Le Cagnard**   **page 76**
    Rue Sous Barri, Haut de Cagnes
    06800 Cagnes-sur-Mer
    Tel. (33) (0) 4 93 20 73 21
    Fax (33) (0) 4 93 22 06 39
    e-Mail : cagnard@relaischateaux.fr
    Website :
    www.relaischateaux.fr/cagnard

14. **La Verniaz et ses Châlets**   **page 82**
    Av. D'Abondance, Neuvecelle-Eglise
    74500 Evian-les-Bains
    Tel. (33) (0) 4 50 75 04 90
    Fax (33) (0) 4 50 70 78 92
    e-Mail : verniaz@relaischateaux.fr
    Website :
    www.relaischateaux.fr/verniaz

15. **La Maison Blanche**   **page 86**
    Place des Lices
    83990 Saint-Tropez
    Tel. (33) (0) 4 94 97 52 66
    Fax (33) (0) 4 94 97 89 23
    e-Mail :
    hotellamaisonblanche@wanadoo.fr

16. **Le Lodge Parc**   **page 94**
    100, Rue d'Arly
    74120 Megève
    Tel. (33) (0) 4 50 93 05 03
    Fax (33) (0) 4 50 93 09 52
    e-Mail : contact@lodgeparc.com
    Website : www.lodgeparc.com

17. **Domaine des Hauts de Loire**   **page 98**
    41150 Onzain
    Tel. (33) (0) 2 54 20 72 57
    Fax (33) (0) 2 54 20 77 32
    e-Mail : hauts-loire@relaischateaux.fr
    Website :
    www.domainehautsloire.com

18. **Le Club de Cavalière**   **page 104**
    83980 Le Lavendou
    Tel. (33) (0) 4 94 05 80 14
    Fax (33) (0) 4 94 05 73 16
    e-Mail :
    cavaliere@relaischateaux.com
    Website :
    www.relaischateaux.com/cavaliere

19. **La Bastide de Marie**   **page 108**
    Route de Bonnieux
    Quartier de la Verrerie
    84560 Ménerbes
    Tel. (33) (0) 4 90 72 30 20
    Fax (33) (0) 4 90 72 54 20
    e-Mail : bastidemarie@c-h-m.com
    Website : www.c-h-m.com

20. Cour des Loges   **page 114**
2468, Rue du Boeuf
69005 Vieux-Lyon
Tel. (33) (0) 4 72 77 44 44
Fax (33) (0) 4 72 40 93 61
e-Mail : contact@courdesloges.com
Website : www.courdesloges.com

21. Les Sources de Caudalie   **page 118**
Chemin de Smith Haut Lafitte
33650 Bordeaux-Martillac
Tel. (33) (0) 5 57 83 83 83
Fax (33) (0) 5 57 83 83 84
e-Mail :
reservation@sources-caudalie.com
Website :
www.sources.caudalie.com
www.caudalie.com

22. Hôtel d'Europe   **page 128**
12, Place Crillon
84000 Avignon
Tel. (33) (0) 4 90 14 76 76
Fax (33) (0) 4 90 14 76 71
e-Mail :
reservations@hotel-d-europe.fr
Website : www.hotel-d-europe.fr

23. Les Hautes Roches   **page 132**
86, Quai de la Loire
F.37210 Rochecorbon
Tel. (33) (0) 2 47 52 88 88
Fax (33) (0) 2 47 52 81 30
e-Mail :
hautesroches@relaischateaux.com
Website :
www.relaischateaux.com/hautes-roches

24. Royal Rivièra   **page 136**
Av. J. Monnet
06230 St-Jean-Cap-Ferrat
Tel. (33) (0) 4 93 76 31 00
Fax (33) (0) 4 93 01 23 07
e-Mail : contact@royal-riviera.com
Website : www.royal-riviera.com

25. Hôtel Lancaster   **page 142**
7, Rue de Berri – Champs Elysées
75008 Paris
Tel. (33) (0) 1 40 76 40 76
Fax (33) (0) 1 40 76 40 00
e-Mail :
reservations@hotel-lancaster.fr
Website : www.hotel-lancaster.fr

26. Les Muscadins   **page 148**
18, Boulevard Courteline
06250 Mougins Village
Tel. (33) (0) 4 92 28 28 28
Fax (33) (0) 4 92 92 88 23
e-Mail : muscadins@alcyonis.fr
Website :
www.chateauxhotels.com/muscadins

27. Hôtel de la Côte d'Or   **page 152**
21210 Saulieu
Tel. (33) (0) 3 80 90 53 53
Fax (33) (0) 3 80 64 08 92
e-Mail : loiseau@relaischateaux.fr
Website : www.bernard-loiseau.com

28. Le Pigonnet   **page 158**
5, Avenue du Pigonnet
13090 Aix-en-Provence
Tel. (33) (0) 4 42 59 02 90
Fax (33) (0) 4 42 59 47 77
e-Mail :
reservation@hotelpigonnet.com
Website : www.hotelpigonnet.com

29. Grand-Hôtel des Bains   **page 162**
15 bis, rue de l'Eglise
29241 Locquirec
Tel. (33) (0) 2 98 67 41 02
Fax (33) (0) 2 98 67 44 60
e-Mail : hotel.des.bains@wanadoo.fr
Website : grand-hotel-des-bains.fr

30. Villa Florentine   **page 170**
25-27 Montée Saint-Barthélémy
69005 Lyon
Tel. (33) (0) 4 72 56 56 56
Fax (33) (0) 4 72 40 90 56
e-Mail :
florentine@relaischateaux.com
Website :
www.relaischateaux.com/florentine

31. Georges Blanc   **page 176**
01540 Vonnas
Tel. (33) (0) 4 74 50 90 90
Fax (33) (0) 4 74 50 08 80
e-Mail : blanc@relaischateaux.com
Website :
www.relaischateaux.com/blanc

32. La Riboto de Taven   **page 182**
13520 Les Baux-de-Provence
Tel. (33) (0) 4 90 54 34 23
Fax (33) (0) 4 90 54 38 88
e-Mail : contact@riboto-de-taven.fr
Website : www.riboto-de-taven.fr

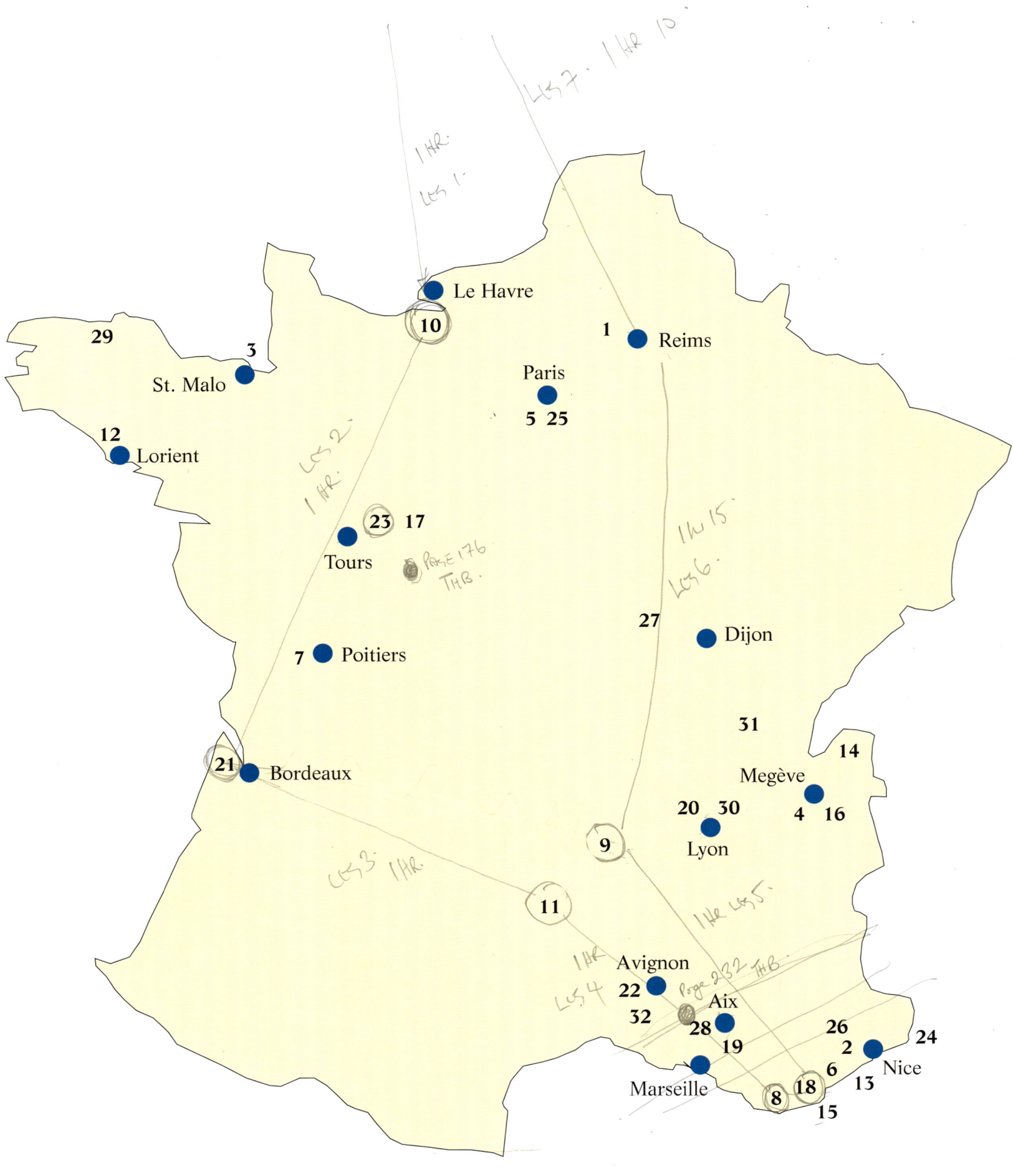

Published in this series

More information on all our books you find on our website :
www.d-publications.com